IT'S A VAMPIRE BAT!

by Tessa Kenan

BUMBA BOOKS™

LERNER PUBLICATIONS ◆ MINNEAPOLIS

Note to Educators:

Throughout this book, you'll find critical thinking questions. These can be used to engage young readers in thinking critically about the topic and in using the text and photos to do so.

Lerner Publications Company
A division of Lerner Publishing Group, Inc.
241 First Avenue North
Minneapolis, MN 55401 USA

For reading levels and more information, look up this title at www.lernerbooks.com.

Library of Congress Cataloging-in-Publication Data

Names: Kenan, Tessa, author.
Title: It's a vampire bat! / by Tessa Kenan.
Other titles: It is a vampire bat!
Description: Minneapolis : Lerner Publications, [2017] | Series: Bumba books. Rain forest animals | Audience: Age 4–8. | Audience: K to grade 3. | Includes bibliographical references and index.
Identifiers: LCCN 2016019654 (print) | LCCN 2016026868 (ebook) | ISBN 9781512425703 (lb : alk. paper) | ISBN 9781512429367 (pb : alk. paper) | ISBN 9781512427622 (eb pdf)
Subjects: LCSH: Vampire bats—Juvenile literature. | Rain forest animals—Juvenile literature. | Bloodsucking animals—Juvenile literature.
Classification: LCC QL737.C52 K46 2017 (print) | LCC QL737.C52 (ebook) | DDC 599.4/5—dc23

LC record available at https://lccn.loc.gov/2016019654

Manufactured in the United States of America
1 – VP – 12/31/16

Expand learning beyond the printed book. Download free, complementary educational resources for this book from our website, www.lernerresource.com.

Table of Contents

Vampire Bats Drink Blood

Vampire bats live in warm places.

Many live in rain forests.

Vampire bats

are mammals.

They can fly, walk,

and run.

They can jump too.

Vampire bats live in groups.

The groups are called colonies.

Colonies can have hundreds

of bats.

Why might vampire bats live in groups?

Baby bats drink milk from

their mothers.

Adult bats drink blood from

other animals.

The babies are ready to hunt

after three months.

The bats sleep during the day.

They hang upside down in caves.

That is how they sleep!

Vampire bats fly out of their caves at night.

They need to find blood to drink.

The bats have sensors on their noses.

The sensors help bats find blood.

The animals bats hunt are their prey.

How would life be harder if this bat did not have sensors?

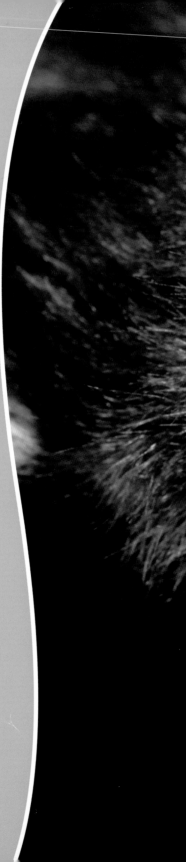

Vampire bats have sharp teeth.

They bite holes in their prey.

They lick up the blood.

How are a bat's sharp teeth helpful?

A bat's prey does not die.

But it can get sick.

Vampire bats can spread illness.

Parts of a Vampire Bat

nose

ear

teeth

wing

body

Picture Glossary

colonies

large groups of animals that live together

mammals

warm-blooded animals that have fur and give birth to babies

prey

an animal that is hunted by another animal for food

sensors

things that can find something

Index

Read More

Arnold, Tedd. *Bats.* New York: Scholastic, 2015.

Mitchell, Susan K. *Biggest vs. Smallest Things with Wings.* Berkeley Heights, NJ: Bailey Books, 2011.

Ringstad, Arnold. *Rain Forest Habitats.* Mankato, MN: Child's World, 2014.

Photo Credits